P9-EEA-004

CALLIGRAPHIES

ALSO BY MARILYN HACKER

TRANSLATIONS

MARILYN HACKER

CALLIGRAPHIES

POEMS

W. W. NORTON & COMPANY
Celebrating a Century of Independent Publishing

For information about special discounts for bulk purchases,
please contact W. W. Norton Special Sales at
specialsales@wwnorton.com or 800-233-4830

Manufacturing by Lakeside Book Company
Book design by Charlotte Staub
Production manager: Louise Mattarelliano

ISBN 978-1-324-03646-3

W. W. Norton & Company, Inc.
500 Fifth Avenue, New York, N.Y. 10110
www.wwnorton.com

W. W. Norton & Company Ltd.
15 Carlisle Street, London W1D 3BS

1 2 3 4 5 6 7 8 9 0

JUN 1 3 2023

For Karthika Naïr, for Nahed Badawia,
in memory of Fadwa Suleiman.
And for Beirut.

CONTENTS

CALLIGRAPHIES

Montpeyroux Sonnets: 2021

Village gone silent in pandemic mode.
School's closed. One small girl with a bike is out.
The narrow street recedes into its doubt
of baker, butcher, neighbour. On the road,
cars rarify, whisk by trees that explode
in redbud, apple blossom, presage fruit.
"Have you had your first, your second shot?"
Masked conversations shrivel into code.
When I was here last, I could walk three miles
back to my histories in Arboras,
sweater in backpack, if the wind turned cold.
I could see people's faces. Chatter was
about elections, new café, roof tiles.
When I was here last, I was not so old.

When I was here last, I was not an old
wolf enclosed all winter in a cave,
no pack, no steppes, no prey, who didn't starve
except for conversation. I unfold
memories like a blanket, stained with mould,
out of some cupboard. Today, I can save
what I'll remember, click my phone. I have
a hundred shots, almost two years I hold
in my palm. On a rooftop, garden shed
clutter, heat, noon, all stun me to be still.
A worker's laugh below scratches the silence.
Two languages, two books, stay shut, while in-
stead of reading, I let sunlight fill
the question/answer blanks inside my head.

The question/answer blanks inside my head—
numb feet, blood pressure—get in the way of care,
joy, generosity. I am a bore.
Age is a bore. Thinking of it's a dead-
end street, huis-clos, a tertiary road
that stops out in the middle of nowhere
at a mound of dirt, under a bare-
bone-blue sky, tyre-tracked. It might have led
out to the mountains, to a different town
where people, unmasked and miraculous,
eat and drink, talk to strangers face to face.
Twilight estranges a familiar place.
Grey clouds look bloodstained as the sun goes down
on autochthons, on refugees, on us.

On autochthons, on refugees, on who-
ever averts her eyes from sun and dust
in the glare of nearly noon, a bus
spatters pebbles passing, one of two
that stop here daily. Within the blue
noon light, everything pauses, bikes, upthrust
iris spears, the bakery, the post
office. The desultory interview
two bored old men conduct goes on, laconic
questions/answers unchanged in a decade.
It's an excuse to speak, rendezvous made
behind masks now, grudgingly, still, a choice
to be incensed, jocular, ironic,
to have a face, have memories, a voice.

To have a face, have memories, a voice,
lowered in conversation over wine
or coffee, in a semi-public place.

To stop in Uniqlo because that jean-
jacket would fill a nonexistent space
in the closet. To take the bus. To take the train . . .
but I did, fled Paris, builders. The only noise
my mind's contagious clangour, its refrain
repetitive. No sandblasting. No drills,
only the fretting and the self-reproach,
which has a name, depression, and seeps back
despite late-morning sunlight on the hills
whose ovine clouds recede as we approach,
driving to Friday market in Gignac.

We drive to Friday market in Gignac
in Julie's car, recuperating years
of spring and summer villages, house-shares:
two beds, one kitchen, somebody's notebook
out on the terrace. It's my turn to cook
dinner . . . Now is now. The omnipresent wears
us down, but market plenitude still cheers
us up. Strawberry season. While I pick
up two punnets, Julie chooses blettes
—and they'd be delicious with cabillaud.
Apricots, almonds, ginger, and should we get
a poulet rôti anyway? As if it were
the same. Everyone's masked. Laden, we go
back through the cobbled sidestreets to the car.

Back down the cobbled sidestreets to the car,
a week later, under cold spring rain,
with blettes, fresh tuna, strawberries again,
and not a lot to say. Perhaps we are
fraying at the edges of a year
where nothing but uncertainty was certain.

Only my fight or flight nerves were alert in
the market square, its plenitude, its cheer
diminished, masked. Don't handle fruit. Don't chat
with the girl selling fromages de brebis
or the fishmonger. Thinking separate thoughts, we rode
past mountain vistas looking oddly flat,
past vineyards, to the empty streets of the
village gone silent in pandemic mode.

Calligraphies I

Younger, we hoped for
long conversations with wine,
multiple passports.

I won't even mention love
and all its accoutrements.

There were wars and wars.
We thought our bookish voices
loud as explosives.

Then we met the others who,
younger or older, were there.

**

Were there memories
that could be re-examined
and made coherent?

In the fug of the café
that seems smoky without smoke

she would like not to
masticate old grievances
but find a hard bright

stone in the evening that
would be afternoon in June.

**

Would be afternoon,
be a walk to the river,
beside or across,

would be a book that opened
to a point of departure.

Meanwhile it's raining,
it's the end of November,
dusk at five o'clock.

There's the ringing in your ears.
There's the splatter of the rain.

**

Rain splatters on the
round café table warmed by
overhead heat lamps.

Three years since she exhorted
the young insurgents of Homs

her dark hair cut short
wrapped up in a keffiyeh
that wasn't hijab.

Not hungry, she lights up her
roll-up, writes in a notebook.

**

Wrote herself a note
with seven o'clock coffee:
what to remember:

awake in panic before
the grey inflected to day

thinking, I'm old and
not working and not learning,
never mind "alone,"

picked up the novel she had
put down at midnight, read on.

**

Read in a Hamra
café, *L'Orient–Le Jour*
juxtaposes war

and students homesick in France.
Assassinations up close,

remembered like a
long dinner with relatives
in adolescence.

Vultures, uninhabited
high-rises on the Corniche.

**

Boys on the Corniche
with wooden shoeshine boxes,
mostly refugees,

while others out on a pier
fishing with a grandfather

are spending Sunday
cementing generations
without lacunae.

Headscarves and lush eye makeup
on two young women jogging.

**

Two women exchange
emails in the fogbound dawn.
One is in Mosul,

armed men at checkpoints on the
highways going anywhere.

One is in Beirut
where anarchy's liberty
she'd wish for her friend.

When she wants to cross the street
she walks in front of the cars.

**

In front of the cars
a grizzled man plies his trade,
not begging, handing

out calligraphed sourate cards.
To pay him is charity.

Was he in Ghouta
two years ago, a thriving
sidestreet grocer,

or here with his prayers through the
war and the war before that?

**

The war before this,
who were the invaders, what
language did they speak?

Were we killed by the known or
the incomprehensible?

Were we familiar
as their brothers and mothers
or calligraphy

in a book they could not read?
When is murder literate?

**

Literate enough
to follow a poem with
a dictionary

and write down the roots of all
the ninety-nine names of God,

not to decipher
some truth from a newspaper's
scrimshaw fioriture,

pass untoward yearnings in
calligraphic contraband.

**

Contraband books for
a library in a tent,
improvised classroom.

Five boys and four girls under
ten intone their alif-ba.

Light bathes the day's text
on a formica table.
Seated facing it

a boy refuses to draw
the home he is forgetting.

**

Husband, wife, at home
in striped cotton djellabas
face each other and

their two little laptop screens
at a round damasked table,

meeting their deadlines
with urban borborygm
beyond the panes where

thin dark construction workers
grapple up the scaffolding.

Ghazal: Arabic

For Agha Shahid Ali

Their roots untwined, the verbs unwind in Arabic.
The poem scrolls down with its rhyme defined in Arabic.

One little vowel, the doer is the done-by:
betrayals can be more refined in Arabic.

Here are a dozen words I could read yesterday—
if my mind goes blank, have I lost my mind in Arabic?

A velvet shadow on a declaration,
a metaphor that was left behind in Arabic.

Have I illusions of recovered youth,
my eyes unblurred and my cheeks unlined in Arabic?

Write in the language spoken by the neighbours—
linguistics of the double bind in Arabic.

The Syrian lady from Cairo described rare books
in Achrafyieh, as we dined, in Arabic.

The little exile opens a third-hand reader
whose politics are unaligned in Arabic.

What did the olive tree say to the bulldozer?
an exercise I was assigned in Arabic.

I wrote a page. The title was in French,
the text in English. It was signed in Arabic.

Calligraphies II

Self-referential,
a text that explains itself.
Al-Mutanabbi

known by pen, night, desert, sword.
My horse and my notebook think

what I am thinking
through an orgy of cadence.
I loved one woman

whose heart gave out when she read
my letter, that I'd return.

**

He could not return:
price on his head, defector.
His mother, with whom

he talked about books on Skype
through bomb-shattered nights in her

once-tranquil suburb,
was going, not back to the
mountains, not Beirut:

road of the insurrection
in her cells. Could not return.

**

Obsessive return
to the site of departure
or abandonment:

checkpoint south of Reyhanli,
a bar in the rue Charlot—

something changed for good.
She got up and walked away.
A guard waved them through.

And the next day and the next
were going to be different.

**

It is different
waking in the city that
used to be your home.

You are what you are, knowing
you are not that anymore,

as old as your friend
when he wrote his late pages
sparring with Bashô

while his sorrel-haired muse fixed
his lunch, pining for cities.

**

The question of lunch,
whether a parenthesis
of conversation

in a cheerful public place
(Tah Marbutah, Hamra Street),

exiles and expats
eating maqdous and kibbeh
in three languages,

or standing near the fridge with
labneh, two verbs, and a spoon.

**

At least two verbs for
departure, five for desire,
come swiftly to mind

from her schoolgirl lexicon.
And all the horses, learned when

she was younger, hoped
to ride away on this new
alphabet, across

deserts of habit and waste
through the six-vocabled dawn.

**

Rainy-fingered dawn
prods the grimy scaffolding
outside the window.

Wet slate roofs, blurry slate sky
swell the list of erasures

you count down, waking.
A sea north of the morning,
a wind from elsewhere—

idea of departure, and
an overstayed welcome.

**

She has overstayed
her transit visa more than
six weeks now. She was

refused a work permit, but
she goes daily to her class,

translates as-Sayyab's
rainsong with them to English,
not their first language.

No news from the Ministry
of Labour. War news from home.

**

A long walk home down
the mango-and-sari street,
then the boulevard's

cheap phone cards to Sénégal,
small real estate agents who

upscale old buildings
pricing the immigrants out.
I'd rather live here.

I'd rather live anywhere
than in my worn-out old skin.

**

Under bruise-red skin,
the Pakistani mango's
sweet wet orange flesh,

mix it with labneh in a
blue-purple bowl from Konya—

where your Kurdish friend
said he'd first heard Rumi
in his mother tongue.

All of you sharing treasures
that no one bequeathed to you.

**

He's inherited
another histrionic
refugee. Curses,

silently, his friend, lavish
with others' time and ideas.

Thinks of his uncle's
trek from Lodz to Liverpool
thanks to a letter,

and calls a man who knows a
man in the right ministry.

**

Give the right answer
in the right tone of voice to
the right person who

ate the right thing for lunch and
drank the right dose of caffeine:

you may walk out with
the right papers to claim your
identity card,

your day relentlessly, you
might say, self-referential.

Ghazal: Myself

They say the rules are: be forgotten, or proclaim myself.
I'm reasonably tired of that game myself.

I watched some friends rush off, called by the wild,
and stayed home to make coffee for the tame myself.

Did sex ever seem like work to you?
Sometimes, five minutes after I came myself.

There are actions I was pressured or seduced to,
but for omissions, I can only blame myself.

Do I think that my averted gaze
nullifies suffering? First of all, I maim myself.

Although I'm manifestly "not my type,"
the one in my bed this morning was, all the same, myself.

Not Elektra, Iphigenia or Clytemnestra,
I'll remain an unsung keeper of the flame myself.

Burnished oak surrounds a rectangle of glass
at the top of the stairs, in which I frame myself.

A signature hangs, unwritten, below the last
line, in which I'm obliged to name myself.

Calligraphies III

Fifty years later
the Ravensbrück survivor
got out her notebooks.

The Gestapo seized her trunks
of thesis chapters with her.

They were lost. She lived—
not a Jew, a resistant.
Ninety, she rewrote

dialogues from the Aurès
under the tents or the stars.

**

Under freezing rain
we walked back from the film, up
the rue de Charonne.

The doctor turned journalist
was an old comrade of hers,

got out of prison
a year before she did, but
he served sixteen years.

What choice? And now? We argued
to the women's shelter door.

**

Shelter of a book
and the lamp's upholstered swath
across the pillow.

Midnight-lit in a window,
a young man washes dishes

in his underwear.
His girlfriend watches the news.
The summer moon's full

of memory and presage
above the same old rooftops.

**

Same old swollen gums
in Beirut, New York, Paris.
Antibiotics

and a dentist appointment
providential in August.

Sick and tired of sick
and tired. Which minor ailment
is a harbinger?

What about the clear azure
and the solar palm of noon?

**

If the cupped palm
held a capsule to suppress
remorse and regret

for words not written or said,
for inert acedia,

would you swallow it
and forget what you might have
done if you were not

nibbling the short hours away,
mired in the mire of your days?

**

Days of translation—
how many words will you keep
and use them again?

Your friend doesn't want to speak
her mother tongue any more.

Not loss of love but
necessity, a new life
in a new language

and nine square meters, not walls
of books, bright kitchen, garden.

**

Told in a kitchen
as she diced a red onion;
read in a kitchen

while rice swelled on the fire;
argued out in a kitchen

over coffee cups
from different hemispheres—
remembered kitchens,

their yellow or brick-brown walls,
their transnational garlic.

**

A bulb of garlic,
six rust-gold shallots, and ten
russet potatoes.

Coins, words, above my cloth bag.
"Your words heal my heart," said the

bearded greengrocer,
maybe twenty. "Egyptian,
by his accent," my

brother from Isdoud told me
as we walked home from market.

**

The common market
turns into Fortress Europe.
Tiny Kurdish boy

washed up on a Turkish beach
whose family name was changed

"Shenu" to "Kurdi"
like the "Israels," "Sarahs"
who, with their lost names,

were, if lucky, refugees
seventy years earlier.

Pantoum

For Fadwa Suleiman

Said the old woman, who barely speaks the language,
"Freedom is a dream, and we don't know whose."
Said the insurgent, who is now an exile,
"When I began to write the story, I started bleeding."

Freedom is a dream, and we don't know whose—
that man I last saw speaking in front of the clock tower
when I began to write the story? I started bleeding
five years after I knew I'd have no more children.

That man I last saw speaking in front of the clock tower
turned an anonymous corner and disappeared.
Five years after I knew I'd have no more children
my oldest son was called up for the army,

turned an anonymous corner and disappeared.
My nephew, my best friend, my second sister
whose oldest son was called up for the army,
are looking for work now in other countries.

Her nephew, his best friend, his younger sister,
a doctor, an actress, an engineer,
are looking for work now in other countries
stumbling, disillusioned, in a new language.

A doctor, an actress, an engineer
wrestle with the rudiments of grammar
disillusioned, stumbling in a new language,
hating their luck, and knowing they are lucky.

Wrestling with the rudiments of grammar,
the old woman, who barely speaks the language,
hated her luck. I know that I am lucky
said the insurgent who is now an exile.

Calligraphies IV

Eight in the morning.
The old woman down the hall
is playing Fairouz.

Grey rain stains these slanted roofs.
Beirut smothers in sandstorms.

The drunkard implores
his neighbour's pretty daughter
not to forget him

in the grand old woman's song.
Down the hall, she sings along.

**

A hall of closed doors
locked on possibilities,
a hall of mirrors,

each reflection is grotesque.
Frontiers are rediscovered

and fenced with barbed wire.
My grandfather's language and
the one I plug at

shouted at each other, un-
comprehending. Mirrors, doors.

**

The morning mirror
is a window on the rain—
early October

like winter in this city.
At the desk in pyjamas,

sorry for yourself,
with dictionary open
to hopeless desires,

you write a word, close your eyes,
hear footsteps diminishing.

**

Diminishing light—
still dark at six, six-thirty,
beige gauze blinds down.

The café has its lights on
as it did five hours ago.

Read for half an hour
in bed, or grab a sweater,
run a bath with foam,

then coffee, newspapers where
daily the darkness augments.

**

My bald friend augments
the ages of all women
his age or older,

writers, teachers, his colleagues.
"She must be at least eighty."

"No, she's sixty-eight
if that makes any difference."
"No, she's not sixty,

she's fifty-four, like you are."
(And his girlfriend's twenty-two.)

**

Two surtitle screens,
English and French. The actors
act in Arabic:

the sack of Ur; scribes, tablets,
the scholar martyr who read

and translated them.
Fadwa knows half the actors,
slips back toward real life

amidst gongs, lamentations,
murdered words resurrected.

**

Resurrected day—
July's late afternoon walks
to reconsider

the unfinished, unstarted,
all the way to the canal.

Three more hours of light:
you could start, you could finish . . .
That was then. Now dusk

deepens before seven, and
late afternoon becomes night.

**

Bright fall afternoon
to walk to the Mairie with
a sack of towels,

shirts, three backpacks, for the bin—
collection for refugees.

You wouldn't offer
your friends two-year-old cashmeres.
In cafés, they won't

let you pick up the bill, and
say "Next year in Damascus . . ."

**

At this time of year
new classes take their form for
teacher and student,

proofs to read for spring issues
while mailing the just-printed fall.

I emigrated,
mark the seasons without a
work permit. So I'm

a student again, translate
three ways, begin forever.

**

Whoever you were,
I'll get used to your absence.
Dinner companion

of a decade and a half,
her wit silenced at ninety;

loves of my life who
decided otherwise, now
something else, or gone . . .

yesterday's brown eyes or green,
yesterday's future now past.

**

Now, figs in salad,
cut up, or figs in labneh,
green Italian figs,

and blue-black Provençal figs
from the three brothers' fruit stand.

Remember figuiers'
branches overhanging stone
walls, or the time we

climbed a ladder to the roof
and picked the late figs of Vence.

**

Vence in September:
on the terrace with Marie,
we heard the ravine

murmur its prelude and fugue
to our reticent breakfasts—

coffee, bread and jam.
She was fifty-nine, and I
was thirty-seven,

that is, almost the same age
as we turned to our day's work.

**

A sonnet turns from
affirmation to question,
landscape to closeup,

a routine doctor's visit
from a chore to a verdict.

The week-old child turns
in her safe wooden cradle
on a Kurdish rug

where a stork feather weaves its
distant song through her morning.

Nieces and Nephews

And because the rain
Has come to live on a hill in the suburbs ...
SA'ADI YUSSEF,
A Fleeting Hallucination

In July, when Tsahal was bombing Gaza
and we marched, and there were flags and brawls,
Lamis waited for me on the corner, smiling
in a lime-green sleeveless dress, not her daily jeans.
There were three cop cars parked in front of my building
and Lamis shouted giddily in Arabic
"She's the terrorist, here!" I pinched her,
shushed her, laughing "Half those cops are Arabs!"
We went to a café, drank wine. She told me
her niece had finally been freed from prison
in Damascus. She lit up her cell phone
to show me the nineteen-year-old girl's photo.
The second of her older sister's children.

Naima's Ismaël on the Corniche, sunlit
in a rust corduroy jacket, white shirt open
at the neck, smiles next to his aunt in paisley
hijab and movie-star dark glasses.
Wind scuds the waves beyond. Out of Mosul
for the first time in his life, she, out of danger
for the first time in six months. The last
checkpoint, the last baksheesh, the abaya
shoved into a suitcase. A walk on Sunday,
a future open as the wine-dark sea.

I drank wine in the same café with Fadwa
last week, at midnight, talking about meters—
blank verse, alexandrines and al-mursal—
though she was keen to go outside and smoke
in the insidious slant winter rain.
"Have you heard from Lamis? I haven't seen her
in a month, she didn't answer an email."
"Her nephew," said Fadwa, "died in prison.
He was tortured." The first of those five children.

I'll meet Ismaël in Beirut with Naima.
In Beirut, no one arrests the daughters
or the nephews of the neighbours these days,
so she can bitch and moan about the neighbours
and how her students can't translate as-Sayyab's
"Nothing but Iraq . . ." The rain is falling
on all the suburbs where it lives in exile
and Lamis isn't answering the phone.

Calligraphies V

Late fall, near midnight,
walking home alone from a
loquacious dinner,

I saw, heard, cop cars, sirens,
thought: There's a big fire somewhere.

Japanese tourists
descend from buses now, take
attack-site selfies.

Illegal demonstrations.
Terrorism: déjà vu.

**

Déjà vu, hard rain
after unseasonable
blue bright mornings.

You Google whom you once loved:
wedding photo at fifty,

face, body, thickened,
shrunk, out of your fantasies.
And what would you say

who said so much once over
those neutral restaurant tables?

**

Winter's not neutral:
damp infiltrates bronchial
passages. You've coughed

since that Burgundy Christmas
pneumonia, twenty years past.

But light's coming back.
But a medical student
blew himself up in

a square in Sultanahmet
where you've been a tourist too.

**

She's been arguing,
she's fed up with rhetoric,
easy amalgams.

You dip bread in olive oil,
then dip it in the za'atar.

Back from Geneva,
with comrades at peace talks that
aren't going to happen—

You proofread her news-brief, see
how her frayed shirt is ripping.

**

Attention fraying
in late afternoon light, soon
day will be done, not

the work incumbent on it
—whatever that might have been—

Gnarls of an old text
in the other alphabet:
can I unknot them,

reweave a mirror fabric
of the unraveled phrases?

**

A day unravels
that she, he, they spent waiting
in line in rain in

administrative limbo
or the emergency room.

Are you immigrants
or political exiles
or refugees? Words

with different valences in
subliminal translation.

**

Liminal space where
exiles with dictionaries
lose themselves: barzakh,

Arabic isthmus, the span
from death to resurrection

in Farsi: limbo,
where Socrates murmurs to
unbaptized babies

in contrapuntal cognates
they hear fardous, paradise.

**

Infantile, senile,
when I read out loud I stop,
stammer and stutter

then pronounce everything wrong.
An illiterate lover

worse than the peasant
accents of emigrants who
return years later

to the villages where their
mothers did not learn to read.

**

My mother would read
to me—fables, fairy tales—
until one Sunday

I said I could read them my-
self, and I did. I was three.

My mother would read
my notebooks, search desk drawers
while I was at school.

I had to tear up and flush
my revolts down the toilet.

**

Down the rain-splashed street,
try not to keep your eyes down
while the sky weighs down

on the wrong side of winter.
You don't forget you aren't young.

Still, there's arrival—
the desposeidos' priest
makes time for welcome,

more liminal narratives
over midnight bacalão.

Ghazal: Your Face

Half-shadowed in the cloudy afternoon's half-light, your face
across from mine—whatever's wrong, that's right: your face.

Framed in bronze-blonde, dark-cropped, curled silver incarnations
I've contemplated, like an acolyte, your face.

The face of the war correspondent taken hostage
resembles, but it isn't quite, your face.

Blotches and spots, the omnipresent wrinkles,
multiply overnight, each night, to blight your face.

A paisley headscarf focuses the eye and frames,
doesn't define, diminish, translate or rewrite your face.

Sallow it may be, flushed with shame or effort—
its history's becoming, being "white"—your face.

The bulbous red cheeks, little red mouth, invoking
Armageddon with a doctored plebiscite: your face?

I almost remember how what almost seemed to
constellate darkness was, through that one night, your face.

To measure out one more day's hours, said the old woman,
would be like cutting off your nose to spite your face.

Calligraphies VI

After disaster
(again) in her small skylit
sublet, N. simmers

lentils while she reads a long
book about Ibn Arabi.

In prison they made
chess pieces out of chewed bread.
She taught the women

to play. Their first champion was
an apolitical thief.

**

Political grief,
apolitical despair,
or it's vice versa—

either way, insomnia.
Rapping on the neighbors' door,

three in the morning—
no, it's seven, and still dark.
One of the roommates

next door home from a night I'm
too tired out to imagine.

**

Imagine language
after opaque years
become transparent . . .

since the hour needs witnesses
who can construct a sentence.

Which was my country?
A schism in the nation,
slogans on banners

while a compromised future
slouches towards investiture.

**

Towards light again, when
wet snow is falling on the
January sales.

The chestnut stairs gleam, but
I'm short of breath, knees give way.

My ideal reader
doesn't read English, and I've
stalled in her language

—or his—while he/she stares at
an impassable border.

**

Bored or despairing
or enduring a headache,
and humid winter.

A book I loved; a reproach:
You read like a three-year-old.

The masters dying,
their festive midnight children
blown out like fireworks.

A constriction in the chest.
An explosion in the street.

**

One Hundredth Street sun-
lit on election morning:
another country

that seemed possible again.
I went to the Baptist Church

to vote—lines, laughter,
scowls, polyglot commotion,
then, fresh air. That night

I read Hannah Arendt till
bad news muddied late daybreak.

**

Bad news for heroes
chain-smoking across borders,
not out of danger.

She smoked outside the café—
it drizzled as we read her

piece for *an-Nahar*;
rolled cigarettes at demos
between her speeches.

She writes in the ward bed with
a chemo port in her chest.

**

Not a port city
but the river is always
lumbering through it

on its muddy way elsewhere,
banks erased often by rain.

We crossed a bridge in
a shurba of languages.
History trundled

beneath, gravel on a barge,
ground down to its origins.

**

Ground beef sautéed with
onions and tomatoes, then
add frozen okra

N. was so pleased that we found
at the Syrian grocer's

near Faidherbe. Why no
okra in Indian food
in France, we wondered?

Bhindi, bamiyaa. A pot of
white rice swells on the burner.

**

Swells and then explodes,
"like a raisin in the sun,"
our impatience, and

others'. Five years ago, in
some café, after some demo,

the Algerian,
Zinab, told the Syrian,
Aïcha, you'll have

what we had, ten black years of
slaughter. And Aïcha wept.

**

Did not cry when I
fell on my face, scraped my chin
and turned my ankle,

or when the midnight and the
morning emails announced death—

a younger man, an
older woman, Berkeley and
Brooklyn, unanswered

letters from two coasts. I took
two pills for my aching face.

**

The two young women
come up the stairs with parcels,
their conversation

punctuated by laughter.
The old woman is coughing

in her apartment.
One of them opens the door.
They can't, she can't know

their white nights' precipices,
her dictionaries' questions.

Ghazal: The Dark Times

Tell us that line again, the thing about the dark times . . .
"When the dark times come, we will sing about the dark
    times."

They'll always be wrong about peace when they're wrong
    about justice . . .
Were you wrong, were you right, insisting about the dark
    times?

The traditional fears, the habitual tropes of exclusion
like ominous menhirs, close into their ring about the dark
    times.

Naysayers in sequins or tweeds, libertine or ascetic,
find a sensual frisson in what they'd call bling about the
    dark times.

Some of the young can project themselves into a Marshall
    Plan future
where they laugh and link arms, reminiscing about the dark
    times.

From every spotlit glitz tower with armed guards around it
a huckster pronounces his fiats, self-sacralized king, about
    the dark times.

In a tent, in a queue, near barbed wire, in a shipping
    container,
please remember ya akhy, we too know something about the
    dark times.

Sindbad's roc, or Ganymede's eagle, some bird of rapacious
   ill omen
from bleak skies descends, and wraps an enveloping wing
   about the dark times.

You come home from your meeting, your clinic, make coffee
   and look in the mirror
and ask yourself once more what *you* did to bring about the
   dark times.

Ce qu'il reste à vivre

I waste the hours still left to me of life:
laundry, bronchitis, weightless messages,
perpetual distraction of the news:
disaster with explanatory graph,
a photo, survivors' shock and disbelief,
multiplied hourly in two languages.
I nurse my conscience, old child nursing a bruise.
Distress, desire, dismay, digression, grief
for the improbable. A passion turned
to an exchange of trivialities,
while crucial friendship dribbles out long distance.
A revolution where the cities burned
made the insurgents into refugees
and bare survival saps all their resistance.

And then it seemed survival meant resistance
to the unspeakable—its blusters, threats,
simian menaces and caprine bleats
(unfair to animals), sleepless insistence
that all remain aware of its existence . . .
The splattered incoherence of its tweets
has sullied discourse, silenced our regrets
with fear and loathing. Oh, remember Wystan's
late lively efforts at a tour de force,
inured to politics by words in orders,
echoing Middle English, Greek, Latin, Norse,
that he could, wistful, ludic, rearrange.
The monoglots are having their revenge,
armed at their checkpoints, shutting down borders.

Subletters, roommates, short-term tenants, boarders
in wintry walk-ups of precarity—
unemployed, overage, widowed, refugee
or redundant—senescent hoarders
of lit mags, Libyan dinars, rolls of quarters:
here we are, hunkered down, superfluous.
The times are dark. The dark settles on us.
Disaster's somewhere that they've sent reporters.
It's night at five again. The paisley throws,
still rumpled in the morning's disarray,
would make a Flemish still-life. Write till nine,
but just translations, footnotes, throwaway
opinion, and, more lightly (I suppose),
another postcard about rain and wine.

Another postcard about rain and wine,
grace note in a cacophony of wars,
posted, during a brief foray outdoors
in hovering daylight, in the rain again.
A year of our disgrace is closing down—
so many plurals might define that "our."
"White women have a lot to answer for,"
a friend wrote, smarting, who is neither one.
Ahed Tamimi, Palestinian
resistant, high-schooler, veteran at sixteen,
came at them bare-handed, *a pagan spear
invading* the invaders. Her wild hair
tied back, she looked, in the Israeli courtroom, "white,"
sat in an Israeli jail, last night, tonight.

بدون, you say it, waking in the night,
a heartbeat word, without, without, without
friendship love sunlight fortune freedom—doubt
a constant, like injustice. Down a flight
of stairs, the drilling starts at half past eight,
while, on a screen, an article about
Ahed, her child face as the guard shoves her out
of range, her crinkled mane catching the light
—accompanied by words: eight months in jail,
where she will study, study war some more.
She could be Rachel Corrie's younger sib.
She could be in Suweida or Idlib,
or coming upstairs with bread, milk, the mail,
taking her shoes off when she comes in the door.

As he knelt in the doorway to take off his shoes,
we were already volleying conversation
about . . . for three years, it was "revolution,"
the last Skype, the next night flight, how to be of use,
and what—doctorate, girlfriend—he might lose
to all-night dispatches, three-way translation,
my jade buddha, his imposed vocation,
since he could . . .
           An old and almost stateless Jew's
opinions braided with new verbs for
desire, dismay, a waft of cardamom,
when we'd gone upstairs with the dictionaries.
What's happened to the revolutionaries?
Silence. A conversation that's become
irrelevant, a footnote, an erasure.

Not even a footnote—an erasure
of her name from this memoir by her ex.
I put the book down. We each have our own facts.
Ivory/onyx votive figures, stature
ascending, fill a luminous enclosure,
because her face, hieratic, was like that—
when she wasn't rolling a cigarette
as she scribbled and drank coffee, her composure
the tension of a dancer on a wire,
at once an artist and a prisoner,
extracting a poem from a news-brief
that in my own penumbra I'd translate,
while she, in her exile's elsewhere, stayed up late
devouring hours still left to her of life

Calligraphies VII

For Fadwa Suleiman

While the same rain fell
on suburbs of exile and
motherless children,

whose courage was certainty
whose impatience turned to doubt,

she came in the door
like a comrade, lover, friend,
and took off her shoes—

older than my daughter but
too young to be my sister.

***

Sister of someone
who was forced to denounce her
on television;

pacifist in keffiyeh,
but they got guns anyway . . .

She rolled impatient
exilic cigarettes, wrote
fables of mourning:

the mother tucked the child in
her bed, and slit the dove's throat

***

Slit-throat, cutthroat sun
slashed wrists of early spring rain.
Wolves at a distance

give up verse panegyrics
and howl like politicians.

Is hope a fatal
disease, or was that despair?
The old woman sheared

her grey hair short as a boy's,
kneaded wine in dough like clay.

***

Words were clay and wine,
what I imagined, she knew
by heart, recited.

The boy who'd stood beside her
was a killer now, or killed.

They bore the cardboard
coffin, cardboard clock tower
at a crossing of

Paris streets, where her voice was
already losing context.

***

Not to lose contact,
with what she was, would be, she
played it on TV—

a Lebanese soap about
political prisoners.

Larger than life, she
acts her life while she lives it,
keeps writing the script,

but not the body's misfires,
or defections in the blood.

***

Blood in the orchard,
or a memory of blood,
a song about it:

shepherds in all the stories,
treason in most of your dreams.

Walk in an orchard
where you picked low-hanging fruit
or shook down olives

in another century's
childhood, before departures.

***

How old was the child,
her son, when she last saw him?
Her choice, her story . . .

but it's close to five years now,
the boy near adolescence,

as my daughter was
at twelve-and-a-half, thirteen
in orchards pendant

to other hill villages,
other declensions of loss.

***

I decline to spool out
or wind in someone else's
narrative spiral.

Don't want that poem to end,
cannot know how it began.

Lead weights in my legs—
because I didn't die young,
age caught up with me,

a face to frighten children
with its own terrified eyes.

***

Own my solitude,
its immunocompromised
auto-absorption.

Write emails in her language,
but she isn't answering,

up against the wall
with no windows on the street.
Outside my windows,

spring drains away though a sky
mottled with silvery clouds.

***

Mottled, nacreous
throat of the dove at her throat,
hope and betrayal

in the book to be published—
only poems, just paper.

The chebab cheered their
Joan of Arc. On YouTube she
preceded herself

toward the dovecote of her chest
in a suburb of the rain.

Calligraphies VIII

Wine, then a headache
at four in the morning. Not
Abu Nuwwas' wine,

amorous and excessive.
One chaste glass was enough for

remorse and regrets,
the butyls and the triptans.
Delivery trucks

stall in the possible street,
where hope was, and a future.

**

The colour of hope
was the blue of Fadwa's scarf
draped around her head

close-shaved through months of chemo.
That day we ate grilled turbot

on a bright terrace
as she made bilingual plans,
her son's arrival,

her film, her revolution,
her etched face circled with hope.

**

Circled in farewell
around earth, around absence,
with something to say—

but the last time to say it
to her would have been elsewhere,

M-G's atelier
overlooking trees and the
train ramping over-

ground, on its way elsewhere. Here,
none of us say, she's elsewhere.

**

Didn't say a word
while lovers and friends put their
hands on the coffin

and read hasty texts or sang
anarcho-feminist songs,

there, the ex-lover
twenty-seven years younger
who'd introduced us

(never mind who betrayed whom)
stood in the sunlight in tears.

**

Terrace in sunlight,
tall yellow tiger-lilies,
two wrought-iron benches

but the city gardener
is too frail and aphasic

to sit there and read
or prune, water, weed, transplant
as once she did. Now

she's wrapped, swaddled, lifted, bride
carried over what threshold?

**

Get over the hump,
of estival depression
because there's no plan,

tickets, map, destination,
no companion you're going to

meet in the morning
at the train station, to cross
at least one border,

change your mind and your language
while conversation goes on.

**

Each conversation
with my friend the engineer
refigures her life.

When she came home to find
her computer, nothing else,

had been stolen, she
crossed the border to Turkey
that night, while she could.

Two stints in prison, خلاص!
Four years of exile, till when?

**

Exile prolonged in
a suburban hospital,
incoherent hands,

face of a saint at the stake.
How did they torture Zainab?

Two languages gone,
she drowns in ebb tides of pain
and a morphine fog,

stabbed by the crab in her chest,
choked by the dove in her throat.

**

Sent her a postcard
from the British Museum—
Christine de Pisan,

one from Cairo, a weaving,
Simorgh in paradise tree,

from New York, pigeon
on skyscraper window-ledge,
rumpled, wet, safe—

taped on her kitchen wall, or
tucked into last year's notebook.

**

Seven years ago,
who had mentioned dementia?
She said "Shoot me first!"

laughed, and we went back to ranking
new translations of Sappho.

A hospital bed
in what had been her study:
gown torn off, she lies

naked, in foetal position—
no lover's bed, and no saint's.

**

Bed disheveled by
insomnia, I dread and
count down till daylight

when I'll get up, go up the
stairs to the kitchen, pour in

water for coffee,
a teaspoon of cardamom
in the filter, wait

as it brews, for not more than
behind the rags of cloud, blue.

**

Fadwa's blue scarf was
buried with her today, draped
over the coffin,

above the revolution's
green white black flag with red stars.

Six chebab, bare-armed,
carried the coffin uphill.
No one was singing

as she did, before that flag,
when a shahid was buried.

**

When N said to me,
frank, not sad, "I don't know you,
and you don't know me.

We talk in a language that's
not my mother tongue or yours,"

I was standing at
the counter, with a wineglass,
dicing aubergines,

while she sat at my kitchen
table, and drank the same wine.

After Forty Days ('Arbaoun)

She called you "My lovely," as you writhed, dying
in atrocious pain that the morphine top-ups
eased for half an hour, and I thought of Tadmor
where you had comrades,

but the Darwish lines I memorized with you
where a mother sings for her martyr's wedding
weren't where I wanted them, on my tongue, if
words could have reached you.

It's too easy to costume you as Zainab
led in chains to Damascene exile (you were
Damascene by adoption, missed the city
more than Lattakié).

Exile, first your refuge, became your torture
as the months passed, added up years, a window
fogged with possibilities gone nostalgic
despite your fierceness . . .

so you chain-smoked, as you harangued who'd listen
on the public squares, in a foreign language,
or spoke softly, friend at a café table
writing your own roles.

How his face, or hers, changed as you evoked it,
wiping dust and steam from a winter window,
the beloved, nameless beyond erasure,
multiple, murdered.

You became your distances, grew your hair long.
Eyes dark-circled, books stacked on shelves behind you,
you said, pale, three times, in dialect: I'm a
refugee, لاجئة

Calligraphies IX

The beloved dead
are gone, could not be more gone—
only the death stays,

only shards of daylight on
their definitive absence.

Today as I walk
up the rue de la Roquette,
January sun

will last perhaps two more hours
of this brief late afternoon.

**

Afternoon of light,
following what was not a
morning of roses:

dog-work, apprentice-work, chores
extricated from the news,

from remembered names
and their mutable faces,
from exile's roll call.

So, clementines, persimmons,
candied ginger, cardamom.

**

Language, mind-candy—
how, not what, it means—
lose yourself in it,

in the roots and the branches.
Once, it was medieval French.

Girl with no Latin
as explanatory bridge,
the words weren't strange,

as I climbed through the stories
with a tress as a ladder.

**

Her fingers stress the
taut strings' memory, the schooled
precise outlaw voice.

She composed the music. Some
of the audience doesn't

speak her language, but
the youyous of those who do
warm the hall as the

long song ends, homesick, recoups
what the qanun remembers.

**

Remember longing
when it was legitimate,
remember writing

in an emerging language,
given words by desire for

what? To still be young
in a world not besotted
with its oligarchs?

The dogs the wolves and the doves
slip into the woods, fly off.

**

Slipcovers of rain
slide over roofs and windows.
Round black umbrellas,

individual dark clouds
cover pedestrians' heads.

No resurrection
in the winter rain after
summer's funerals,

no long walks down shopping streets
talking past five métro stops.

**

Past Nujoom Chaussures,
La Boucherie de la Paix,
Franprix, Monoprix,

I head home from Belleville (the
street of my old editors)

down the hill to the
Place de la République, where
we sat with candles,

roses, photos, rebel flags—
heartbeat of heartbreak, بدون.

**

Without much purpose
on an overcast morning,
turn to translation—

Why should this brilliant young dyke
be seduced by abstractions?

Never mind, it's my
first other language, I can
whittle suggestions

of what might or could not be
uttered into filigree.

**

The Filipino
man from the wine shop downstairs
is shoveling snow.

It's the first day of March, it's
one of the longest winters.

I've brought in four of
the geraniums, and the
hyacinths I hoped

would last through the early spring
—they'll bloom, die early, hothoused.

**

Brisk early morning,
vendors and beggars are
already at work,

windy day between winter
fog and estival excess.

The old woman with
a red silk scarf from Halab
sits in March sunlight,

drinking pomegranate juice,
looking out on Hamra Street.

**

Tonight Farid's out
in a bar in Mar Mikhaël
where people know him,

but it isn't his real life.
He left that behind in Homs.

With no work permit
Amina is stir-crazy.
Their daughter will leave,

take her new nursing degree
and find work, not "if"—when, where.

**

When I was six, I
wanted to be a shahid.
We were communists,

I knew already there was
no heaven, just my country.

When I was nine, I
wanted to wear hijab. My
father said "You're not

leaving the house like that!" I
only held out for two days.

**

Out on the Corniche,
you raise your voice above the
wind, tide and traffic,

to read her words out loud in
the language they were meant for

while two headscarved girls
in ardent conversation
pass, and ignore you—

saying, beyond erasure
the names of the beloved.

Calligraphies X

Like Jude the Obscure,
you wait beneath the vaulting
of a corridor

where you never belonged and
nothing here belongs to you.

How sallow your skin,
how outmoded your clothing,
how crumpled your face,

while multiethnic students
stroll past, bright-caparisoned.

**

How bright the past looks,
when that was being forty,
free, in an airport

on some Adonic journey
or in a more recent year

believing in the
revolution you kissed her,
kissed him away to—

Kafranbel's Friday demo
recounted to you in French.

**

The French woman who
can't go back to Damascus
shouted at her friend

the activist refugee:
The Kurds were right to keep out!

Now it's civil war!
The two Kurds—one's her husband—
said nothing. Around

us on the lawn, families
heard Arabic, and wondered.

**

I wonder about
my friend in Jerusalem.
Imru al-Qays is

his muse, if you will, and he
translates Palestinians.

A scholar my age,
protests what former exiles
inflict on exiles,

but why that street, that hill, in
all the diasporic world?

**

Diasporic grave,
narrow as a ploughed furrow,
elbowed in on both sides

by riverains of Montreuil
who lived and died there, while she

was housed there by chance:
political refugee's
right to a lodging—

accidental neighbourhood,
now her accidental tomb.

**

Tadmor tomb portraits,
the person's name and "Alas"
beside his, her face

in the little museum
in Hamra, empty today

brother and sister,
a distraught-looking lady,
a husband and wife,

Palmyra, empty today.
Khaled al-Asa'ad: Alas.

**

Antigone was
a role for her, and I know
she played the part

in Arabic, as I saw
it played in Saint-Denis by

Palestinian
actors. In Damascus, she
was in a theatre.

Then they were outside, the stage
built in haste, the words her own.

**

There was a word I
didn't know in your letter,
almost a friend's name,

one character different. I
looked it up, and it means death.

The rebel who tied
her wild hair back to speak at
Fadwa's funeral

is gone, forty-nine, no one
quite knows how, why. Some love kills.

**

Some lovely useless
ubiquitous foreign word,
bougainvillea

blooming well into July,
framing blue vistas of sea.

An orange cat walks
by. There are hundreds, not strays
but the descendants

of civil war survivors
abandoned in this barzakh.

**

Stacked in abandon
of any order but what
might catch the eye, books

you now imagine reading,
al-Jahiz and al-Ma'arri

and here, this woman
an essay revealed to you,
dead too soon, poems

a dictionary lights up
as you probe among the roots.

**

If Abiah Root
had kept writing letters to
her friend Emily

after she moved to Beirut,
and if Emily wrote back . . .

Amherst to Beirut—
birds of imagination
circle the Corniche,

invisible ink quatrains:
where, *with them, would harbour be?*

Ghazal: الجندل الصمّ

فيا لك من ليلٍ كأنّ نجومه
بأمراس كتّان إلى صمّ جندلِ
What a night when the stars seem
Bound to the deaf rocks by cords of linen
IMRU AL-QAYS, MU'ALLAQA

A line of salt like a linen thread is wound to the rocks.
Wave-break, boys singing, gunfire—make no sound to the rocks.

If God blessed vegetation, fish, birds and beasts,
then humans, did s/he get around to the rocks?

Shout your rage in the din of seaside traffic.
Whisper the thought you thought was so profound to the rocks.

They dug a tunnel to go under the border,
why did it only lead them underground to the rocks?

Doglike, the waves bring the cadaver
of one more boy from a rubber boat who drowned to the rocks.

The spectre of an ancient woman comes striding,
haggard and magnificently gowned, to the rocks.

At ritual's end, someone is carried,
stark naked or caparisoned and crowned, to the rocks.

Andromeda became a constellation,
but Princess, even the stars tonight are bound to the rocks.

Listen

I hear the words that I was born to listen
to, though it makes my guts churn to listen.

The inarticulate patient has words for pain.
Who'll teach the overprivileged intern to listen?

Walk into the foreign circle. Say something,
though I would rather be silent. I yearn to listen.

My mother was too angry at her grief
and too determined to be stern to listen.

I write stories, but the language hasn't claimed me,
And it won't, until I learn to listen.

Imagine, when you find your words and speak your words,
the Beloved will stop, for once, and turn to listen.

Oligarch, you bellow you'll bomb their cities.
They say: then your city will burn too. Listen.

"You gave me language, and my profit on't
. . . . . . is that you taught the subaltern to listen . . . . . .

Pantoum with Trombone Player

The sun is a disaster waiting to happen,
The gypsy trombone player starts to blare
La vie en rose again, and *Hello, Dolly.*
I turn Fairouz up not to have to listen.

The gypsy trombone player starts to blare,
today, and yesterday, at noon, at seven.
I turn Fairouz up not to have to listen,
and hear my panic clanging in a cavern.

Today, and yesterday, at noon, at seven,
the sun in splendor, summer, and it scares me.
I hear my panic clanging in a cavern
where light and dark are blaring repetition.

The sun is splendid, summer, and it scares me—
the pain and disappearance I came back to,
where light and dark were blaring repetition,
replay—their names, their unforgiving absence.

The pain and disappearance I came back to,
the absent present, and that present absence
replay their names, their unforgiving absence,
their works and words dispersed in summer's rubble.

The absent, present in a present absence,
remind, reproach, revoke the possible,
their work and words dispersed in summer's rubble,
their human presence strained through pain and finished.

Remind, reproach, revoke the possible
boys on scooters, girls on bicycles,
their human presence strained through sun and finished
dispersing in the glare of noon and traffic.

Boys on scooters, girls on bicycles,
messengers of an annunciation,
disperse in the glare of noon and traffic,
drag a chilly dissonance behind them.

Messengers of an annunciation
that will not be of birth or celebration
drag a chilly dissonance behind them.
The phone will ring, or there will be a letter.

It will not be a birth or celebration,
La Vie en Rose again, or *Hello, Dolly.*
The phone will ring, an email, or a letter.
The sun is a disaster waiting to happen.

Ghazal: This Winter

Above the gables and the lamps a hunter's moon this winter,
clear as a lightbulb or a polished spoon this winter.

Awake at five, awake at six, awake at seven
the light is gone, and not returning soon this winter.

Spit in a cup, hold out your arm for the needle,
blow out hard as you can into a balloon this winter.

"To write a sonnet is a fascist act"—
Suggest that to the next tyre-burning goon this winter!

The slave girl stole the king's mare and rode away—
write her آيات, her canticle, her rune, this winter.

After you left, I didn't know for the last time,
I listened to an exile play qanun this winter.

Acedia, bronchitis, despair, nostalgia—
diseases to which I'm not immune this winter.

Oh, weren't we once gallant and outrageous?
Now we trade ailments on the phone, ya Mimijune, this winter.

Let's say that the beloved's name is Shams
For it is Shams I am بدون. this winter.

Ghazal: تخلُّص

It's dark at six, at seven middling-grey out.
The day begins drawing its long delay out.

Carpets and cushions, still a prison cell
of absences—open the door, go out and stay out.

A whiff of spring and ocean in the wind
brings joggers and dog-walkers on the quai out.

Protestors unfurl banners on the square.
Cops on the sidelines wait—how will it play out?

The corner café's prices geared to tourists
keep students from the neigbouring lycée out.

"*Fucking guidebooks!*" In mind, I cross its name
(it used to be my go-to pause-café) out.

Resigned, like Proust's grandmother after dusk, make tea,
and take the *Letters* of Madame de Sévigné out.

Beneath the zarb, threading the tar's lament
I tease the lyric commentary of the ney out.

Who chose the rhythms, dug the roots of words?
Who'll hear the hapless verses that I pray out?

The windowpanes at night still look like jail—
I sign my name as if my name might be a way out.

Calligraphies XI

Fayza said to me,
"During the day, I'm happy,
lonely when it's dark."

She's fifty-something, in a
tiny walk-up in Belleville,

and made us kebbe
with pomegranate syrup,
hummus and fattouche.

"When night falls, I'm alone with
solitude." Claire, ninety-three.

**

Nine months of illness,
a year away from Beirut,
of *timor mortis*

at six on summer mornings
awake in sweat-crumpled sheets.

Now with departure,
a duffel bag of trouble
on your mind again,

you sort out the books and clothes,
throw the unused pills away.

**

Used clothes and used books,
past years packed in shopping bags
for charity shops

to diminish the clutter,
to make room for the clutter

of too many books
just bought, and clothes from the *soldes*
as if you had space,

as if your years could expand
into numberless chapters.

**

Meaningless numbers,
a birth year, death year, an age,
the months of mourning.

Her engravings on the wall,
her book, and hers, near my bed.

There is nothing in
the buzz of ginger or wine
to pry tomorrow

out of the sunlight's hollow
one-sided conversation.

**

Conversation in
a room, the rain, on a path
going anywhere

and nowhere, and where would you
rather be? Gnarled apple trees,

hydrangea bushes
moon-green in late afternoon,
an old man with keys

to his allotment garden
and a bag of lettuces.

**

Dropped the laundry bag
off where they remember me
from a year ago.

Squeezing my pomegranate
juice, the portly grizzled man

asked: Don't we know you?
Yes, I was here last spring and
two years before that.

Women, the same ones or not,
are begging on Hamra Street.

**

Hamra Street perfume:
sizzling man'ouche, red diesel,
late-day narguilehs.

In one café two bearded
men my age write in notebooks.

I'm not at home, I'm
not homesick, not sure of my
footing and language.

I could learn Spanish in French.
Learn 'amiyeh in fus'ha?

**

If I order it
in fus'ha, the waitress smiles,
brings my glass of wine,

understanding how much I
entirely don't understand.

So much forgotten
of noun roots, branches of verbs
I scratched in notebooks

for weekly hours when nothing
or everything could go wrong.

**

"Old's" the wrong gender,
like being the only girl
on a team of boys,

wrong race; the one black or
brown student in a white class,

entirely alone
if there's a problem and you're
in over your head

or too reticent to ask
in your old-lady wolf suit.

**

Wolf of solitude,
oud in late October wind,
wolf words at wolf-hour.

Is there a revolution
not routed or turned riot?

Too tired or too late,
in always the wrong language,
but I'd howl in it

intuiting what he meant,
not repeating what she said.

Corniche, Pink Dog

Walking between the city and the sea,
I passed a group of old guys, shirtless, pink-
chested, playing cards. And then a dog

scurried by, a scraggly, sniffing dog,
as ordinary as you'd ever see—
but someone had hair-dyed it shocking pink

as the bald pelt of that Rio stray, the pink
nursing bitch Bishop addresses in Pink Dog,
expatriated, near a different sea.

I snapped it. See, there's always a pink dog.

For Marie Ponsot, Remembering

To bring you back, Marie, at least to me,
as we were, brilliantly not old or young,
above the ravine, on a Manhattan street, among
friends, among strangers, in dialogue, blessed were we
among women, prayer you hid for all to see
as title of what might read as a song
chafing at limits, but that would be wrong,
though there's no reading that was wrong entirely
to you, who'd give what anyone might find
your full attention, if it had been paid.
What attentive elements remained
in the half-locked box of an aphasic mind—
green words burgeoning in a green glade,
monastic multiparous solitude?

Multipara, monastic solitude
seemed sometimes like the object of desire,
or *was*. Teresa, mind inconveniently on fire,
on muleback, between convents, understood.
A convent once, a cabin near a wood
years later . . . thesaurus, notebook, the entire
sky and its swooping denizens. You require
just enough water. You forget about food . . .
Back in the world of marriage and divorce,
you observed, listened, wouldn't supervise
composed and decomposing families.
Once, with spiral notebooks on our knees,
Petrarchan sunlight getting in our eyes,
we sat for hours near the unsounded source.

For hours they'd sit near the unsounded source,
knowing, despite crossed wires, it all was there—
determination, something like faith, despair
refused like blasphemy. You couldn't force
language, why would you, when it might traverse
your mind unasked. You'd lost the words to the Lord's Prayer
in English after the first stroke. It appeared
in Latin, on mental parchment—which, of course,
you back-translated, for quotidian use
in mind, at midnight, in a hospital.
A nicotine patch brought back Pascal
as gallstones brought you closer to Montaigne,
body's and mind's uncompromising truce,
that long-ago July in Avignon.

Beijing, London, Houston, Avignon,
postwar Paris; change, better or worse.
Queens childhood, many childbirths, a long divorce,
a long apprenticeship on each horizon.
There was always something to improvise on—
new alphabet, Tang statuette, red horse
on a cave wall, collaborative verse
while wine poured alongside the running dragon.
I stop the way you stopped when you composed
those tanka, riffed on your own words, weeks apart,
a blue jay, a blue ashtray, and you'd start
writing, crossing out, writing, ten minutes or
five hours on a couplet or a metaphor,
then you coughed, looked around you, notebook closed.

One day you closed the notebook, left it closed.
Was all the "after" after that an afterthought,
after what you learned, after what you taught,
the languages and strategies you used
to stay abreast, erect, alive? You posed
"with a rosetree up your spine" once, caught
in someone else's image. But you sought
and found your own. You still sat straight. You dozed
between visitors, between internecine
battles. You hated war. You'd loved. They'd died.
After your youth of Latin verbs and wine,
you classed detritus from a battlefield.
The junk of war, the junk of love, revealed,
turning the coin, your face on either side.

I turn the coin, your face on either side:
absolute loss, absolute composure—
and wonder what we knew about each other,
if I misunderstood choices you made.
We were complicit, decade after decade,
wordsmith, itinerant, polyglot, mother.
There was no rupture, there was no closure
but absence, incomprehensible, denied.
I was across the always-defining ocean
that changed your life, that keeps rewriting mine.
Monique made what's unbearable routine,
and gentled it, so that you could remain
your self-contained, observant self, pristine
in dialogue with all and anyone.

Your dialogue might be with anyone,
the uncertain young, infants, the wild old
—or so you hoped they'd be, taught and enthralled
by grandmothers, nuns, grocers. Free electron
at a kitchen table, on a night train,
stalled on your terrace in the March chill, shawled
and silent in a wheelchair, as you recalled
to view illuminations in your brain
that you might not enunciate again.
Misfired synapses were tragedy,
whose syntax once cohered in poetry,
whose unsaid subtexts no one will explain.
No cognate phrase parsed in this foreign rain
will bring you back, at least to me, Marie.

(Marie Ponsot, poet and teacher, 1921–2019)

Ghazal: يا لطيف!

A lot more malaise and a little more grief every day,
aware that all seasons, the stormy, the sunlit, are brief every day.

I don't know the name of the hundredth drowned child, just the names
of the oligarchs trampling the green, eating beef every day,

while luminous creatures flick, stymied, above and around
the plastic detritus that's piling up over the reef every day.

A tiny white cup of black coffee in afternoon shade
while an oud or a sax plays brings breath and relief every day.

Another beginning, no useful conclusion in sight—
another first draft that I tear out and add to the sheaf every day.

One name, three-in-one, ninety-nine, or a matrix of tales
that are one story only, wellsprings of belief every day.

But I wake before dawn to read news that arrived overnight
on a minuscule screen, and exclaim يا لطيف every day.

Makdisi Street Calligraphies

For Fady Joudah

Wine fucked up my sleep,
one glass of white Obeidy
with dinner for one,

the pile of dictionaries
pushed aside on the oilcloth.

Alone or not, I
sometimes drink that wine, sleep well.
The oud-playing wine

merchant on Souraty Street
smiled, small wry affirmation.

**

Three small beggar girls
danced and clowned in front of the
hotel manager

having a smoke on the steps.
He joked with them, had them guess

which hand held some coins.
One dashed into the lobby,
and was chased out. Two

ran in again. He took off
his belt, lashed. They fled, laughing.

**

Rain lashed the terrace,
generator ziggurats,
air ducts, washing lines

one kitchen window lit up.
Clouds scudded past a half-moon.

Awakened by drops
on the panes, February
storm that might bring spring,

I looked at my watch in the
penumbra, four-thirty, day.

**

The hundredth day of
the intifada, awake
hours before فجر

too stressed to be resisting.
No revolution, only

ginger-cinnamon
tea by the window, curtains
pushed aside to watch

five street girls run past, shouting
"The people want the fall of . . ."

**

People linger on
the Corniche, kids ride rented
bikes, Sunday fishers

on the rocks. February
sunlight already feels like

spring, could recede
back to rain and riots.
Now, garrulous light.

Sea behind her, a woman
in niqab takes a selfie.

**

Borderline self,
outside a revolution
season that's changing

no one knows yet into what.
It's late for more rain. The boy

on the roof across
the street—autistic, maybe—
there daily, pulls his

sweatshirt hood over his head,
stares down at the puddling street.

**

Down Makdisi Street
the revolutionaries
are banging on pans

and chanting. Monday morning,
maybe the banks will open

and students will get
to school, despite roadblocks
or being locked in

their rooms so they won't join
the street cortege banging pans . . .

**

Wash the frying pan,
all the coffee cups, plastic
take-out containers,

decide what to pack in the
swift-departure duffel bag

what to leave behind,
thinking of Fadwa: "our ink
will be attar and laurel."

Never returned. Wager in
the fridge: half-bottle of wine.

Ghazal: أطباء القلب

Halab, Qamishli, Isdoud, for Ovid, once Rome—in the heart
of exile, one name remains home in the heart.

There are some stones and a small pile of ash in the desert.
There is the silence beneath a magnificent dome in the heart.

I look out at a three-quarter moon after three weeks' confinement
that daily inflames a desire to roam in the heart.

Not every old lady—but some—looking frail in the market
or too stout on the bus, has an insolent môme in the heart.

The bad gene for cancer I probably got from my father.
My blood pressure rises from which chromosome in the heart?

Such palpitations, and all of them augur departure,
throbbing beneath the unmarked aerodrome in the heart.

What's the djinn in my mind makes me want what I shouldn't?
I created that golem, invited that gnome in the heart.

Silenced, the call to فجر, the first bell of matins,
in my cloister still start up the same metronome in the heart.

يا أخي، يا أختي your faces look out on all four chambers.
If I am not honest with you, there's no poem in the heart.

Ghazal: Beirut

Each year it opened a parenthesis—Beirut.
Street kids shine students' shoes on a street called Bliss—Beirut.

My lips are, they'd say, much too old for kissing,
but no one was too old to kiss Beirut.

Odor of za'atar on street-stand ma'anouche sizzling,
of uncollected garbage and of piss—Beirut.

To buy a book, you have to interrupt the old guys'
shisha and political analysis: Beirut . . .

Coffee with her, with him, at noon, at midnight,
and extra hâl for emphasis—Beirut.

Walked to Gemmayzé, bickering like lovers
or siblings, would it always be like this, Beirut?

Gemmayzé, then, was bougainvillea balconies,
stories, survival, photosynthesis, Beirut.

Politicians, plague, not jealous angels,
hurled you from heaven like Ibliss, Beirut.

No calligraphy, my hand's in plaster,
بس أنا مشتاقة, I miss Beirut.

Ghazal with a Radif Taken from Charles Bernstein . . .

I was up at dawn reading the *Graun* on election day.
My airmailed vote was back in my hometown on election day.

People preferred a modest man to lead them.
The autocrat would have preferred a crown on election day.

Often enough, you have to show your papers
to cast a ballot if your skin is brown on election day.

Wasn't there a horror film, where children
take poisoned candy from an evil clown on election day?

Six hundred children in detention centers
or foster homes, whose parents can't be found on election day.

A Kurd from Ilam dove into the churning
waves while his boat sank. He drowned on election day.

The autocrat loosened his tight red necktie.
His wife drank vodka in her dressing-gown on election day.

Protestors marched to the golden tower, turned
their backs to it, and pulled their trousers down on election day.

Alone in quarantine I'm a bad witness.
Was "Change" a verb, or static abstract noun on election day?

Ghazal: Here

Disease, contagion, then restrictions, fear, here,
and isolation, weeks, six months, a year, here?

The café was my small flat's extension,
for meetings over coffee, wine, a beer, here.

September was convivial, a harvest
that burned. Its smoke pollutes the atmosphere here.

When was the last time someone touched my shoulder,
began a phrase, chérie, habibti, dear, here?

I keep music on loud against the silence:
Handel, Fairouz, the voices that I hear here.

There thirty years, chairs piled behind locked doors now.
One morning, will the waiters reappear here?

Walk with someone—the Seine's a different country,
or the Buttes-Chaumont suddenly near here.

I've gone to Monoprix for conversation,
not food: masked words exchanged with a cashier here.

In this city, my private life was peopled
in semi-public space, now there's no "here" here.

Montpeyroux Sonnets 2

A rainy Monday, everything is shut.
It could be late October; it's mid-May.
Lights on at noon, outside rain drums on grey
paving stones, drainpipes, voices. Nothing but
water on roof tiles in a steady beat,
the postman's motorcycle passing by,
not stopping. Tomorrow, the bakery,
grocer, butcher—bread, vegetables, meat,
revivifying possibility
of a "bonjour" exchanged with an unknown
person, whose eyes express the smile,
question, mistrust or curiosity
her or his face mask almost hides, as I
exhale uneasily behind my own.

Exhale uneasily. Behind my own
pretense of standing firmly, I'm unsteady
on my feet, impatient but unready
to take one more step, toward some overgrown
weed-wilded plot. Leaden feet weigh me down
on the empty morning street. Ahead, I
see the post office, clock tower. I buy bread. I
buy a bunch of red onions. The town
is quiet as the plague that got its claws
into the blue-green globe a year ago.
Queasily accustomed to the laws
that change monthly, the shops shuttered because . . .
I make my way, awkwardly lame and slow,
up sloping streets out of de Chirico

Up sloping streets out of de Chirico,
too clean, too empty, garrulous grans indoors,
kids quiet, holiday-rental visitors
quarantined in cities, the status quo
is stasis. Now, here, stays here and now:
curfew, a trajectory that blurs
the border of the ten kilometres
allowed beyond the door. Today, tomorrow,
something will change, the wind, the rules, the weather,
a numbness, swelling, or suspicious cough.
Yesterday, in late sunlight, on an off-
road, a brown horse stood in a field,
flanks aglow in the slant light, untethered
and shimmering in a stasis that seemed wild.

Shimmering in a stasis that seems wild,
unseasonable, unpredictable
as thunderstorms or canicule in April,
the certainty of change. There was a tiled
corridor; the amputated, undefiled
torso of a boy in stippled marble;
a bird that cawed, that whistled, one that warbled;
a sketch of an old man reading, sketch of a child
herself bending to draw a hopscotch grid
near the gazebo on the village square.
I sat on a bench there. I thought of Claire
eighty-two years ago—a similar
village, the same grid, during the drôle de guerre,
not thinking she'd write about it. But she did.

Not thinking he'd write about it, still, he did,
first scribbling birdtracks on a yellow lined
pad—place-names, objects left behind,
in his three languages. He stopped in mid-
phrase (they weren't sentences) as a word fled,
or was it the object, shimmering in mind,
but disappearing, shrinking to a blind
spot with a velvet aura. He shook his head,
rubbed his eyes, squinting, put down the pen,
light pricking them like summer dust that stings.
Beyond the window, a street full of things
in motion, even when they were still.
That wasn't the road leading out of Tell
Abyad, that he was walking on again,

Walking out of the ruined town again,
having gone back to probe the rubble, look
for what was left of the school, the mosque, the book-
shop, where after school daily eight or ten
children would awkwardly appear, and listen
to tales they'd coax from him—he shook,
despite himself. Here was the souk,
or had been. No manouche, no heaps of green
and russet vegetables, no polyester
djellabas, no men, no women, no mercantile
palaver, only an urban vacant lot,
cardboard boxes, dogshit, a scrawny cat,
and plastic bags of household trash on piles
on rubble. I'm not him. But I was there.

I'm not there, probing the rubble. I wasn't there
with cousins in Gaza as the bombs
exploded. Israeli bombs. Agents have names.
I'm not holding the pen that doesn't spare
me. No sleep. The pointless vigils wear
me down. Bad back. Bad conscience. Spasms
drizzle and clutch my spine, and open chasms
of half-remembered mishaps, terror, error.
To walk out through the fields was easier
than through damp city streets that probed my pain
(or joy) sometimes, with something to discover,
translate, transform, enumerate again
at every corner bus stop, shop front. But
it's Monday. Almost everything is shut.

Museum Piece

Once, Phoenician triremes stood in harbour,
poised for merchant journeys of exploration.
Honey, wine, gems, dyes for a purple tunic,
scarabs and daggers.

There were artefacts in the small museum
on the campus nobody ever came to—
goddess statues, bracelets, rings, swords, toy wagons,
Tadmor tomb portraits,

lively, saddened faces, a bit of makeup.
A clay hippopotamus, painted azure:
toy or minor deity?
      The explosion
undid curators'

care as it did doctors', grandfathers', mothers'.
But the feral cats, who survived, as always
bask in light, millennial, the debris of
August around them.

Montpeyroux Sonnets 3

July. The air is thick. I'm out of sorts
with my ankles, knees, wrists, with my spine
that's fusing into something that's not mine,
or not my body, functional. Resort
to pills, to naps, a vegetative state
wanting a summer afternoon again
to walk through fields, and look out at the mountain.
Attractive nuisance of the internet
instead, four countries' daily newspapers.
A stack of books, but I can't concentrate,
be in his mind, craft, story, be in hers.
Imaginary swelling in my feet,
sour stomach, prickling under the short hairs,
the desiccated nerves of lost desires.

The desiccated nerves of lost desires
don't, now, even reweave themselves in dream.
Sometimes I want to want. I want to scream
as if I'd poked my finger in a fire.
In fact, all I want really is to sleep
eight hours, or six, not lie, midnight till dawn,
lamp off, determined not to turn it on,
admit I'm wide awake, and that I'll creep
around tomorrow like an invalid,
afraid I'll lose my credit card, or trip
and break a metatarsal, with my mind
elsewhere, putting down my coffee cup
in the next-door café, the way I did
last year, as soon as we were "unconfined."

Last year, as soon as we were unconfined,
people gathered on café terraces
in all weather. It was May. It was
a warm spring, not a grey one, where it rained
until July. Some people fled on trains
to natal or vacation villages
to stay. There were more graphs than elegies.
There was no cure. There still were no vaccines.
We replaced clichés of solitude—
trees in bud seen from windows, still-lives of food
cooked solo, with the river, a smiling friend,
face mask a bracelet dangling from her hand
and a barge passing in the distance. In
October, everything shut down again.

Mid-October, everyone was out
marching, ambling, downtown on Clemenceau.
The banks banged down their shutters, dropped a row
of steel window-protectors. All Beirut
was bristling, singing. Somebody would shout
a slogan, chant it, someone would repeat
or rhyme it. Women laughed. A toddler sat
on her father's shoulders, waving her sun-hat.
Three little refugees, who'd sit and beg
outside al-Fakhani grocery
where I'd stop for feta cheese or eggs,
in a brain fog from the university,
dashed down the street, their hair flying, and screamed
"The people want the fall of the regime!"

The people want . . . . . Next fall, the same regime
stayed put, but half the city had exploded
in August. On WhatsApp, everyone I know—did
you? Were you? Shattered glass and chaos. Reem
on her terrace as it blew up. Nadim
in a refugee squat in Bourj Hammoud.
In the ER all afternoon, Fouad
triaged . . . what was, what only seemed
life-threatening: two cabdrivers, a grandmother
more concerned with where her grandsons were.
I wasn't there. WhatsApp, email, but not there.
My squares and riverbanks oddly serene,
riverains strolling, dogs, few visitors,
in a parenthesis from quarantine.

Parenthesis between two quarantines—
the morning makeshift grocery-café
on the town square, coffee, a Perrier,
a breeze from anywhere I might have been.
The wrought-iron table in the roof garden,
olive tree, rosebush, fan of hortensia
leaves, same notebook, later the same day,
pale green, green-shiny, splayed green, olive-green:
Julie's creation, but she's far away;
this estival also-parenthesis
now coming to an end. Covid tests, train,
certificates attesting our vaccine
status. Next month, a new government pass.
Tomorrow is the last day of July.

Yesterday was the last day of July—
and so the train, once carefree, gagged in masks.
Bring fruit, a sandwich, water. Last night, with casks
as décor, crisp white in ice-bucket, I
dined one last time on the place. A family,
a couple, eight young friends. No one greets, asks,
and why should they? There are different risks,
excess of solitude, of company.
I brought my notebook, and Germaine Tillion's
pre-war years in the Aurès . . . incongruity
of following her there while nibbling on
filet de bar and miniature desserts,
claiming some solo solidarity.
August. The air is thick. I'm out of sorts.

Montpeyroux Sonnets 4

October 2021

The sun is out, and Julie's still in bed
at noon, at one, one day at half past four.
Another bright October day, one more
spent walking, writing emails, solitude
become habitual, there, here. My mood
depends on the temperature outdoors,
and if the sky is bright or going dour.
I take one of two morning walks, once I've had
mint tea. Coffee, awakening's elixir,
leaves a sour taste in my mouth now, a sour
stomach. Stasis. I wanted change, but not
to stop missing the espresso-pot
left in my Hamra kitchen the day I fled
and become a dyspeptic invalid.

December 2021

Mornings of a dyspeptic invalid—
herb tea and maybe toast. Then down the stairs
to the street. Nobody would be there
but a bored child, an ash-blonde village kid
tossing a ball against a house wall. Mid-
morning, not early. The sun was high. The air
was free of cigarette smoke, bus fumes, clear
as a swimmer's lungs, a mathematician's head.
I miss it in the city's narrow, grey
streets I once wanted to inhabit, more
than I wanted "love and fame." They're my
turf now, my recourse every shortening day.
A hint of winter silver in the sky.
A breath of winter silence at the door.

A breath of winter silence at the door
that doesn't open for someone who kneels
sheds her, his shoes on the runner. Time unreels,
doesn't rewind. Fadwa died young, four
years ago. She isn't anywhere,
least in a cemetery in Montreuil,
exiled from all she never got to say
in either language. The second plague year.
I'm still alive, still vulnerable, older
than when we walked from Bastille to Concorde
and back, recounting, sparring, every word
glistening with possibility. It's winter,
darkening. I take a letter from a folder,
put it back. The door's shut. They won't re-enter.

February 2022

A door closed on the dark. They will not enter
again, who are a dozen forms of gone—
to the country, to another country, on
to a life with other borders, a different center.
Or gone as "dead and gone." What he meant, or
she thought, I won't know. Flute, oud, saxophone,
on a CD, another afternoon
descending into darkness, that inventor
of fantasies and schemes—why not? If? Or?
Also of sleepless nights and phantom pain
rehashing the impossibles, *yes, buts,*
of brand new backaches, twinges, costive guts.
At half past six, I double-lock the door
knowing I won't be going out again.

Knowing I won't be going out again,
I take stock of what's in the fridge, then, wine . . .
Unfreeze the veal chop. I bought that kale, when . . . ?
A bottle of unpedigreed bourgogne
from some populous market morning, one
Sunday I had the energy to ven-
ture out—it wasn't cold; it didn't rain—
stifling behind the face mask I put on
as soon as I was downstairs, on the street.
Masked, I hunted, gathered—winter fruit,
spuds, chard, carrots, broccoli, soup meat,
dried petals of ginger I eat like candy,
hummus, mutabbal—a few words bandied
back and forth, and he half-joked, "Enti min Beirut?"

March 2022

I said, half-joking, "Ana bint Beirut . . ."
after I'd told the driver where my street
was, in Arabic, car il avait une tête
d'Arabe, like half our taxi guys. The route
was roundabout. We reached my front door
via the glitter, ghettos, via chat—
l'Aurès, Algiers, hirak—till I got out
on my street corner.

All the news is war

days later. Shi'a, Sunni, Zionists,
not in this one unless they're in the way
when somebody starts shooting.

I make lists,

not shopping—books and clothes. What I should pack
and what's in Hamra (Katia wrote today)
waiting like cousins for me to come back.

Greeted like a cousin, I've come back
to Montpeyroux, in chilly early spring,
my spine, my circulation, everything
worse than it was a year ago. I lack
hormonal gumption, but I walk, I walk
to Le Barry, La Meillade, achy, breathing
deep, with the mountains in a distant ring
around, with my phone, for photos, in a backpack.
Three women my age, with short grey hair,
stop at the water fountain on the square
with their bikes, on the road from here to Arboras.
At the épicerie, I have a glass
of Perrier, then get two croissants and bread
at the boulange—Julie might be out of bed.

Montpeyroux Sonnets 5

1.
Fug of the canicule. Fug of the aches
in neck, spine, abdomen, ankles and hips.
Fug of the words that don't come to my lips
or mind, to say, to write—to whom? Mind makes
mountains of anthills, lakes of drain pools, slakes
its thirst there, loses its balance, grips
a wobbly railing that's unsteady, slips
and falls this time, clutching the rail that breaks
the fall. But a bad sprain. Now it's truly lame.
The correspondent whom I hoped might read
my letter, poem, postcard, has forgotten
my phone number, address, if not my name.
My mind's sour as my stomach. There's something rotten
in all this undirected, flailing need.

2.
I need good light, a good night's sleep. I need
a moratorium on blurs and twinges.
(I need new glasses.) My body impinges
like age, like the heatwave. I try to read
Yeats again, Adrienne, happenstance, feed
on someone else's bookshelves. Reading binges
once compelled like lust—now, rusty hinges
of my mind creak almost-shut.
                              Some weed
grown scraggly in a parched field, unforgiving
sun, fever . . . Fady was in Darfur,
a doctor, writing, sixteen years ago.
Here's his book. He'd say "That's then . . . "? I barely know

the borderlines of what I'm barely living
through now. Familiar landscape. Feels like war.

3.

Move through familiar landscape. Feels like war
because war's everywhere. No village, highway,
mountain range, shopping mall, not somehow, some way
in Dimashq, Gaza, or Lviv. No door
out of the darkness, door out of the glare
into a temperate place, where people play
chess, tric-trac, gossip. "Damn, it's hot today!"
"Don't you remember the heat the year before
last?" Yes, I remember. I remember, though
I wasn't there, Nahed playing chess
in Adra prison, after she'd taught the rest
of the women to play. In a photo
on my phone, she grins, arms spread, with a glass
of wine, my caption "A happy communist!"

4.
I raised my glass. "A happy communist!"
"Not now!" she said. "At university,
in high school, maybe." Now, democracy,
assimilation. She's on no one's list
but keen freelance employers. I persist
in thinking, some of the others might be free
now too, food shopping , teaching history,
telling a child . . . Unfettered Zainabs. Blessed.
I sit under the ceiling fan that whirs
hot breeze into the heat. Alive. Diminished.
Dyspeptic. Heat-wave silence on the street.
Longing wells up like bile, while vision blurs.

I want this sour acedia to be finished.
I want a glass of something to taste sweet.

5.
I want a glass of something to taste sweet—
Perrier, wine, pomegranate juice, tisane,
cold water from the tap. I want the sun
to be restorative, light, yes, and heat
not keeping shutters drawn daylong. My feet
have lost the memory of roads that run
from town to hamlet, from Belleville to Saint-
Denis—alone, to some improvised beat
of conversation—gossip, argument,
politics, anecdote . . . "Quand j'étais enfant . . . "
Vary the language and fill in the blanks.
When I was a child, I wandered in books,
away from bickering. Found highways, sex
(yes), rhyme, languages. For which I give thanks.

6.
Three languages, for which I give thanks.
French is my alter ego. My Arabic
sucks, but in a funk, I work through text,
and roots, tenses, return, in a phalanx
bearing fruit, not shields. English? The bank's
open all night, my credit's good, the next
payment was made. I think my wit is quick
as it was, well—when it was. Words, like hanks
of chemo hair, fall out, but there are more
words, replacements, substitutes, stand-ins.
I fish for synonyms, antonyms, rhyme,
and some echo, impertinent, begins

a sentence I was almost waiting for,
and I get where I was headed, almost on time.

7.
I get where I was headed, almost on time,
walking on rubber tyres (it feels like), zapped
alert with caffeine, and two or three WhatsApped
messages from Elsewheres, places I'm
still present, absent. We agree, the clim-
ate's a disaster happening. Heat-stopped
to basics, people drank or fucked or napped
the afternoon away. What tastes good? Lime
sorbet, Perrier, maybe an apricot?
Some stretching exercises till the heat breaks
(it's past seven now, and it's still hot)
when I'll walk to the village square, my back
achy from sitting, fingers numb, stiff neck.
Fug of the canicule. Fug of these aches . . . . .

Acknowledgments

Some of these poems have appeared in journals including *Agni, American Poetry Review, Liber, The Michigan Quarterly Review, The New England Review, The New Humanist* (U.K.), *PN Review* (U.K.), *Poetry Northwest, Poetry Review* (U.K.), *Prairie Schooner, Rusted Radishes* (Lebanon), and *Sinister Wisdom.*

"Ghazal: The Dark Times" and "Ghazal: يا لطيف!" were published on the Academy of American Poets' "Poem-a-Day" site.

"Ghazal: Myself" was a Poem of the Week selection in *The Guardian* (U.K.).

"Calligraphies" I–X, "Ghazal: Arabic," "*Ce qu'il reste à vivre,*" "Ghazal: The Dark Times," "Ghazal: Your Face," "Nieces and Nephews," "Pantoum," and "After Forty Days" appeared in *Blazons: New and Selected Poems 2000–2018* (Carcanet Press, 2019).